W9-AUF-350

Opposites!

By J. Douglas Lee
Pictures by John Farman

Gareth Stevens Publishing
Milwaukee

BRIGHT IDEA BOOKS:

First Words!
Picture Dictionary!
Opposites!
Sounds!

The Four Seasons!
Pets and Animal Friends!
The Age of Dinosaurs!
Baby Animals!

Mouse Count!
Time!
Animal 1*2*3!
Animal ABC!

Homes Then and Now!
Other People, Other Homes!

Library of Congress Cataloging-in-Publication Data

Lee, J. Douglas.
   Opposites!

   (Bright idea books)
   Bibliography: p.
   Includes index.
   Summary: Contrasting terms and illustrations use children and animals to depict opposites in things, conditions, and moods. Includes special activities encouraging the reader to respond creatively.
   1. English language — Synonyms — Juvenile literature. [1. English language — Synonyms and antonyms] I. Farman, John, ill. II. Title.
PE1591.L37   1985   428.1   85-25132
ISBN O-918831-94-6
ISBN O-918831-93-8 (lib. bdg.)

This North American edition first published in 1985 by

Gareth Stevens, Inc.
7221 West Green Tree Road   Milwaukee, WI 53223, USA

U.S. edition, this format, copyright © 1985
Supplementary text copyright © 1985 by Gareth Stevens, Inc.
Illustrations copyright © 1984 by Octopus Books Limited

First published in the United Kingdom with an original text copyright by Octopus Books Limited.

Typeset by Ries Graphics Ltd.
Series Editors: MaryLee Knowlton and Mark J. Sachner
Cover Design: Gary Moseley
Reading Consultant: Kathleen A. Brau

Contents

full
empty

4

wet
dry

12

soft
hard

16

23

lose
find

neat
messy

out
in

even
odd

night
day

31

33

brave
cowardly

38

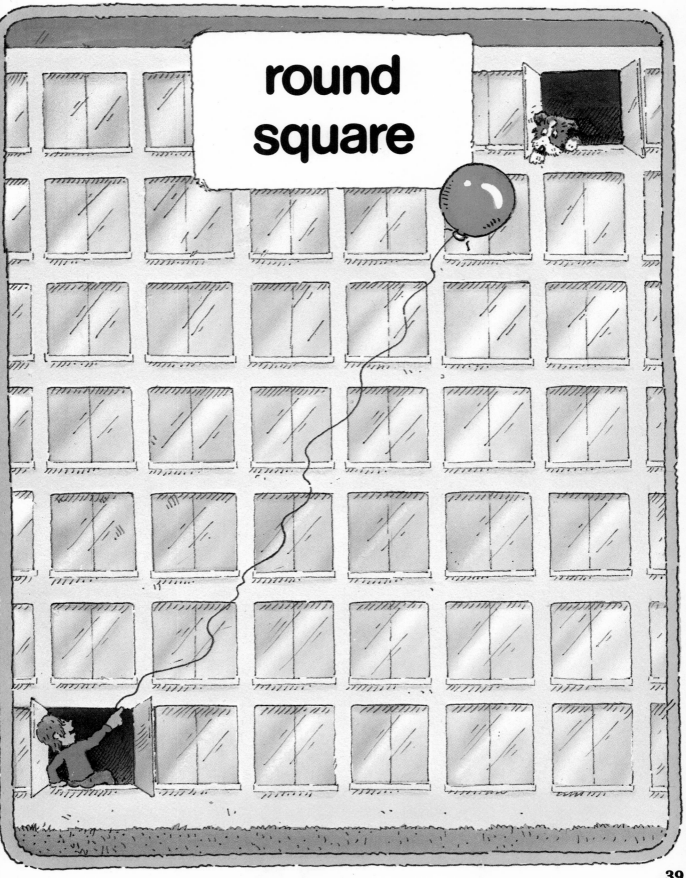

41

above
below

sick
well

Things to Talk About

The following "Things to Talk About," "Things to Do,"
and "Index of Opposites" sections offer grown-ups
suggestions for further activities and ideas to share with
young readers of *Opposites!*

1. Think about <u>opposites</u>. What does the word
    <u>opposite</u> mean to you? Now look around you. How
    many opposites can you see where you are right
    now?

2. Use the Index of Opposites to find
    pictures of the opposites listed below. Can you find
    things in these pictures that are also the <u>same</u>, or
    almost the same? What are they?

    full / empty * happy / sad * tall / short * dull / sharp

3. Use the Index of Opposites to find the opposites in
    the list below. In these pictures, can you find any
    <u>new</u> opposites that are <u>not</u> named? What makes
    them opposites?

    full / empty * happy / sad * dull / sharp
    soft / loud * round / square

4. Use the Index of Opposites to find the opposites
    <u>happy/sad</u> and <u>big/little</u>. Can you find these
    opposites in any of the <u>other</u> pictures in the book?

5. What do you think makes the people or animals
    look happy or sad in the other pictures in the book?
    Now think about how the opposites <u>happy</u> and <u>sad</u>
    happen to <u>you</u>. What things make you most happy?
    What makes you most sad?

Things to Do

1. Write down <u>ten</u> opposites as quickly as you can think of them. Now check the Index of Opposites to see how many of your opposites are in this book.

2. Here is your chance to form some more opposites that are not in this book. Just take out a separate piece of paper and match every word in the left column with the word in the right column that <u>best</u> describes its opposite.

silly	quiet
broken	serious
noisy	dull
rough	closed
tired	narrow
pointed	rested
angry	pleased
open	whole
sound	smooth
wide	silence

3. See how the faces of the people and animals are drawn to show the opposites in this book. Now choose <u>eight</u> of the pairs of opposites you made in number 2 above. Can you make faces that will show what <u>those</u> opposites might look like? Find a brother, sister, friend, or grown-up, and see who can come up with the faces that <u>best</u> show these opposites!

4. Look again at the list of opposites in number 3. Now try to show each of these opposites by using any part (or all!) of your body <u>except</u> your face! Can you do it?

As Opposed to . . . ?: Index of Opposites

More Books About Opposites and Other Words

Here are some more books about opposites and other words. Look at the list. If you see any books you would like to read, see if your library or bookstore has them.

Animal ABC! Lee (Gareth Stevens)
Big and Little. Weigle (Grosset & Dunlap)
Eight Ate: A Feast of Homonym Riddles. Terban (Houghton Mifflin)
Fast-Slow, High-Low: A Book of Opposites. Spier (Doubleday)
First Words! Lee (Gareth Stevens)
High Sounds, Low Sounds. Branley (Harcourt Brace Jovanovich)
New Illustrated Grosset Dictionary. Bennett (Grosset & Dunlap)
Picture Dictionary! Lee (Gareth Stevens)
Simon & Schuster's Illustrated Young Reader's Dictionary. (Simon & Schuster)
Sounds! Lee (Gareth Stevens)
Traffic: A Book of Opposites. Maestro (Crown)
What's That You Said?: How Words Change. Weiss (Harcourt Brace Jovanovich)

For Grown-ups

Opposites! is an easy-to-read picture book that acquaints young readers with the concept of contrasts in things, conditions, and moods. The "Index of Opposites" is, in effect, a controlled vocabulary list of *every* word that is used in the main text (pages 4-43) of the book. The index will give educators, librarians, and parents a quick guide to using this book to complement and challenge a young reader's developing language and reading skills.

The editors invite interested adults to examine the grade level estimate at the bottom of this page. Certain books lend themselves to reading level analyses using standard reading tests. *Opposites!,* because of its format, does not. This concept book helps children discriminate among objects by size, color, shape, and character. The reading level of *Opposites!* is therefore determined not only by how "hard" the words are, but by a child's ability to grasp the subject matter in a visual format.

The grade level span given below reflects our critical judgment about the appropriate level at which children find the subject matter an achievable challenge.

Estimated reading level: Grade level 1-3